The Life God Has For You

Mimi Ajala

To my amazing husband Samuel, who releases me to fulfill the ministry God has given me and supports me with all that he is.

To my beautiful children who I pray will walk in the fullness of the image of God.

Contents

Introduction

It is a wonderful thing to become a child of God. We so often proclaim it to the world, and we sing the songs, but do we know what it means? After praying the prayer of salvation, your Father is now God Almighty, but have you started living a life that reflects this?

Can you say confidently that you are living the life that God has for you as obtained through His Son, Jesus Christ? The Christian faith isn't a slogan; it's a way of life. To be exact, it is a fantastic way of life that shows the heart of God towards all humanity. Your life should reveal the fullness of God. Don't be satisfied with chanting empty regurgitations. Many people live frustrated lives because what they find themselves saying couldn't be further from their reality. You cannot be satisfied with living in less than what Jesus has done for you because you will be missing out on the power of God locked up on the inside of you. There is a phenomenal life packaged with your name on it, but will you open it up and begin living the life God has for you?

You may ask, "How can I live in what I don't know has been given to me?" or, "What exactly does this life look like?" This book will open your eyes to all that is available for you as a child of God, and it will empower you to reject less and push to live in the beautiful and abundant life that God has set aside for you. Your life as a Christian is God's number one tool to show the world who He is and by the truth found in this book, you will become all God is so that the world can see Him inside you.

CHAPTER 1

From The Beginning

Then God said, "Let Us make man in Our image, according to
Our likeness; let them have dominion…" …then
God blessed them…

Genesis 1:26-28

Whenever you want to understand a matter, it is so
important that you go back to the beginning. It is
at the beginning that you will discover the original intention. Therefore, whenever I need to understand God's
design on a subject, I always find that the Holy Spirit leads me
back to the beginning. Often the journey of life causes people to stray from their root; the source that led them to goodness they experience. Traditions come, ideologies form, society
changes and little by little, without the believer realising it, they
too lose their identity and their way of life.

We see this very clearly in today's society. Many people call
themselves followers of Christ but continue to be intertwined
with the ways and ideologies of the world. They have complete-

ly lost sight of God's intention for them to be known as children of God. When God first created man, He had a plan and purpose, and that plan still exists today for anyone that chooses to walk in it. This means that the same life that God intended for the first man Adam is the same life that God has planned for you to live also. Everything that Adam walked in and every blessing that he operated in can be yours and is supposed to be yours. There is no difference between you and Adam. None at all!

God's original intent for man

Let Us make man in Our image

Genesis 1:26

Man was created to be a replica of God; God's very own mini-me. When God made man, He gave man the capacity to replicate God's abilities on earth, which means your prototype was based on God Himself. How amazing is that? When God was designing you, He looked at Himself and copied exactly what He saw to come up with you and me. We see this resemblance between God and man in scriptures.

God is a worker, a creator and an enhancer (Genesis 2:3).

So, before man was formed, God ensured that man's work was created (Genesis 2:5). The first man was created for a purpose and was occupied with his project. Everyone created in the image of God is formed in the same manner. We all have our specific life-long project that occupies us. We see this reaffirmed by Jesus in John 5:17 when He said, My Father has been working until now, and I have been working. Therefore, you are not walking in the life God wants for you if you don't have a something that occupies you. God even bestowed on man His level of wisdom. This was so that God could partner with man on his creation and trust that man had the capacity to finish off the work that He began. Look at this:

> Out of the ground, the Lord God formed every
> beast of the field and every bird of the air and
> brought them to Adam to see what he would
> call them. And whatever Adam called each living
> creature, that was its name.
>
> Genesis 2:19

I find that incredible. Whenever a manufacturer makes a product they sign it off with a name and that name acts as the manufacturer's seal; it guarantees the authenticity and quality of the product. Therefore, a manufacturer would not leave the task of choosing a product's name to anyone whose wisdom does not compare to theirs. God left the naming of His creation to Adam because Adam's wisdom was aligned with His. In other words, God thought Adam had it in him to finish off the work He had started without the need for supervision.

This being called 'man' was created to be incredibly awesome, and this stands true today for everyone that is a child of God. It's not a slogan, nor is it a motivational quote, but a truth that should rule your mind. You are incredibly amazing. Whenever God appears, we are amazed. Whenever Jesus appeared, the people were amazed. When Peter spoke, the people were amazed, and the same should be true for you. Your salvation through Jesus Christ has released the true content of who you are, and you are nothing short of amazing. However, God did not end it there. God then made all that He enjoyed available for man to enjoy on the earth.

Genesis 1:29 to Genesis chapter 2 talks about God supplying all the needs of Adam bountifully. The first man was a man of wealth that could not be limited because his supplies outstripped his needs. Adam had access to resources. This was, and still is, God's intention for all humanity and we have access to that same life now that we are children of God.

How did all this work?

And the Lord God formed man of the dust of
the ground and breathed into his nostrils the
breath of life, and man became a living being.

Genesis 2:7

The power behind the first Adam was God. Man was nothing but a gathering of dust; he had no ability, no capacity and definitely could not do anything close to what God could do until God poured into man what was in Himself. We call it the breath of life. God, Himself is the reason any man can function at the capacity God intended.

God would continue to come down in the cool of the day and spend time with man to pour Himself into man. This fellowship between God and man fuels the power behind man. Adam maintained his capacity and continued in glory as long as he fellowshipped with God.

The effects of sin

We have been led to believe for many years that when Adam sinned in the garden that he lost all his possessions. Yes, he lost things, but what Adam actually lost in the garden was

God Himself:

> Therefore the Lord God sent him out of the
> Garden of Eden to till the ground from which
> he was taken.
>
> Genesis 3:23

According to this scripture, nothing changed in Adam's life except his access to the presence of God. Remember, Adam was created to till the ground, so that was not what changed. What changed was that he was sent away from the source of his capacity, his strength, and his glory.

Gradually, things began to change for humanity. Since sin entered into the world through Adam, we have had to live life far below our means and our capacity. We began to suffer and became accustomed to suffering. Evil crept into our world; he who was created to be mighty had fallen far from his place of grace and glory. At this point, I am reminded of the phrase, "Oh how the mighty have fallen"; to be intended for nothing, but greatness, advancements, and goodness, yet to now live in a state of sorrow and fear of that which you once had dominion over. This was the new normal for man, and many wouldn't even know that it was not so from the beginning. All of it lost because man lost access to the source of his power and his

Maker, God.

If we observe the world in which we live today, we will notice that the more we take God away from our lives, the more evil occurs. The removal of God and introduction of our 'freedom' appears to be an ingenious solution of man but has in fact brought about nothing but confusion and destruction. Many are led to believe that when we walk away from God, we are walking into freedom. That is the same lie your enemy, the devil, sold to Adam and his wife. Walking away from God and His principles cost them everything, and it continues to have the same impact on people who choose that same path today.

Any freedom that does not have boundaries will lead you into captivity. A man and a woman who decide to have an open marriage because they want to experience freedom always find themselves hurt, broken, damaged and destroyed. That lie opens the door for every evil work of your enemy, the devil. Where the original intention for a thing is ignored, it cannot be used with total freedom. It has been designed to function in a particular way and under certain conditions. If you continue to operate outside of the instruction of the manufacturer, all you will end up with is frustration. However, following the guiding principals of the manufacturer will allow you to enjoy the creation at the highest level: total freedom.

Proximity to God is our greatest asset. Our life is in His breath and without which we are merely dust of the earth. We were designed for a specific life and a particular dominion. However, all of this is accessed through continued closeness with God, our Maker. It is through this that we will mirror Him and become like Him. It is in the continued proximity that we become everything that we were designed to be. You were not created to be subject to this world and live a miserable life. You should not, therefore, continue to live that way, especially when your Maker has come up with a solution to restore you.

God's solution

It amazed me to discover that many Christians still do not understand the role of Jesus in the life of a believer. For the majority, Jesus Christ died that we may go to heaven and avoid the terror of hell. It will surprise you to know that there are multitudes out there who if told by God that hell did not exist, would be satisfied with the earth and have no interest in heaven.

The moment Adam stepped outside of God's plan for all of us and allowed the devil to take dominion of the earth in his place, it grieved God. God is so filled with love for us, not just as His creation but as His children. His heart is burdened by our living below the standard of life which He freely provided.

I come from a nation with a royal family. How do you think the Queen would feel if she saw her son, the Prince, struggle through life as a mere civilian when he has the entire kingdom for his comfort? All the resources of the territory belongs to the Queen, and she and her family enjoy the full benefits of them. God takes no pleasure in seeing us, his children, live on the peripheries of the life He designed for us. So immediately God came up with the solution of Jesus. God decided to take on human form and destroy the reign of the devil and the curse that came upon all humanity through Adam's sin.

Some say, "Well, I am a good person." It does not matter how good you are. Sin is your natural state because you are born of Adam and are of flesh and blood, and that sin disconnects you from the presence of God. As long as you are not in the presence of God, you are living under the curse of the devil and sin. Adam lost it all and put our inheritance in the hand of our enemy, the devil. He gave the devil the earth and put sin in us, so we could not come near God.

But your iniquities have separated you from your God; and your sins have hidden His face from you so that He will not hear Isaiah 59:2.

Jesus (God with us) came and lived the example of the life that God had in mind for us from the beginning. He came to tell us that it was not supposed to be what we have become accustomed to and to show us a more excellent way of living. Finally, Jesus dealt with the cause of our problem, which is separation from our God.

The Bible tells us in Matthew 27:46 that when Jesus was on the cross and our sins were upon Him, He said, My God, my God, why have you forsaken Me? He was now in our place, separated from the presence of God. However, suddenly we start to see the beginning of victory in verse 51 of Matthew chapter 27, Then, behold, the veil of the temple was torn in two from the top to the bottom.

This appears to be random. What has a veil got to do with Christ's death? That veil was the separation of all humanity from the presence of God. Until the veil was torn, only one person had access to God's presence once a year. The High Priest, after appropriately atoning for his sin and the sin of the people, would obtain preservation for God's people for the upcoming year. It was behind the veil, in the presence of God, that the High Priest would collect the fuel and power from God to elevate God's people to that glorious life that God intended.

However, by Jesus, the veil was wholly destroyed, and we no longer have to be separated from God our Maker. This means that as long as we believe in the death and resurrection of Jesus Christ, we have total access to the presence of God all day every day. Access to his presence now means that we are changed from glory to glory (2 Corinthians 3:18), elevated continually into that sure glorious life that God intended for you and me until we reach its fullness. Every time you go into God's presence, you become more like Him.

CHAPTER 2

The Believers' Rights

...For all things are yours...

1 Corinthians 3:21

T he death and resurrection of Christ is the anchor of our hope and victory as a believer. For us, it means that He won. It says that the battle that we lost in the Garden of Eden, where we gave up the glorious life of dominion that had been designed for all of us, is now available to anyone who believes in the finished work of Jesus. By this victory, everyone who believes that Jesus Christ died and rose again for them has the right to live in all that Adam once had access to. Jesus restored us to our original place, and that place is a place of dominion over the earth. When man was in his place of dominion the earth served him, but from the time the devil deceived Adam, man served the land; living subject to it and it needs.

Remember how in Genesis, God, after creating man, bless-ed man and commanded him to have dominion? Well, that means that life shouldn't be a perpetual struggle in the hope that one day you may be rich. Life should not be lived in fear of death and sickness. You should not take the hand that you've been dealt and manage. It is not just that some people are lucky. God did not design you to be left to chance. We are designed for a guaranteed life. Look at God, and you will see that there is no one and nothing more sure, more stable and more in control than Him; everything works together at His command. This is the way it is supposed to be for you.

God said, Let Us make man in Our image, in Our likeness. There is nothing that can happen without His command. As He wants it, He speaks and it is so, which speaks of unquestionable authority. You have the same power Jesus displayed during His stay on the earth. Even the fish brought forth real money when He required it; the earth served His needs rather than binding Him in fear and uncertainty. Now that you are a believer in Jesus Christ, you can live like that also. Whatever the original man had, or however he lived, you can now live like that because Jesus has taken back all that was lost and given it to you. You should no longer live subject to the curse of sin and operate in the fall of man because you have been rescued and therefore exempted.

Examine your life now, and should there be anything around you that resembles the fall of man, you now have the right to walk out of it. That thing does not have the right to be in your life, so don't tolerate it. Don't just go for some, make sure that you live in all (including the most insignificant of them all) that Christ has obtained for you, some of which have been listed in Revelation 5:12:

> Worthy is the lamb that was slain to receive power and riches, and strength and honour and glory and blessing.

Think of it like this: a prince was kidnapped and given to a family in poverty. When his royal family found him, they destroyed those who had abducted him and restored him back to his place in royalty, but that prince continued to live in poverty. The prince continued to go hungry when there was a butler beside him and would dress in rags, despite the rails of expensive garments in front of him. Anyone who observes such a prince would rightly label him insane.

The Bible says in 1 Corinthians 3:21, All things are yours including the world (paraphrased). Therefore why would you continue to live like you have nothing? The entire earth is at your disposal. Please do not allow the enemy to somehow live in victory over you when in fact his battle was lost to your saviour on your behalf. In Colossians 2:11 - 18, Paul instructs the believer to ensure that they are not cheated out of their reward. Why? Christ has removed everything that is contrary to your design and make-up that is causing you to live below your capacity and authority. Christ publicly embarrassed everything working against you; He has made you triumphant again.

What does this mean?

It means that though we are in this world, as believers, Christ has made us no longer of this world. Therefore, we do not suffer as the world because the laws that govern it do not rule us. The most important thing for you is to discover who you are. Where you are from determines who you are. Who you are is determined by where you are from. Where you are from determines what rights you have. Let's take a look at Colossians 1:12-13

> ...the Father who has qualified us to be partakers
> of the inheritance of the saints in the light. 13
> He has delivered us from the power of darkness
> and conveyed us into the kingdom of the Son of
> His love... Colossians 1:12-13

Philippians 3:20 goes further to state that our citizenship is in heaven. It doesn't matter what gloom is happening on the earth; your portion is different. God gives us a foretaste of his agenda with the children of Israel in Exodus 8:22 (NIV):

> But on that day I will deal differently with the
> land of Goshen, where my people live…

That speaks of no evil being permitted around the children of God. God's mindset is what should set your expectation. A believer will always live like a mere man if they live by the standards of this world. Jesus throughout his earthly journey would announce the Kingdom of God has come near to you (Luke 10:9, Matthew 12:28). This is the focus of our salvation; we belong to a different world and have a different ruler. What a glorious life you have the opportunity to now live: to live like the royalty you are, to live like the ruler you are and to live like the god you are.

Psalm 82:6 states that ye are gods, and all of you children of the Most High. The problem is that people want to experience all of that without believing that Christ has done that for them. It is impossible to live in that restored dominion if we refuse to believe that it is Christ that has enabled us to do so. Jesus Christ was the one that died, battled with the enemy (the devil) and won and collected all that was stolen from mankind. He then rose from the dead as a witness of the victory obtained. Jesus Christ did all of that, not us. So we must now hide under Christ so that we can receive all that He possesses.

Therefore, in Galatians 2:20 Paul informs us of the secret to his life of dominion and victory: I have been crucified with Christ; it is no longer I who live, but Christ lives in me; and the life which I now live in the flesh I live by faith in the Son of God, who loved me and gave Himself for me. Once we take this same approach, we can live in God's original plan for us. We can become all that we were designed for; residing above all principalities and obstacles that once ruled us.

The place of your faith

But as many as received Him, to them He gave
the right to become children of God, to those
who believed in His name

John 1:12

All that I have mentioned previously hangs in the balance of your faith. It is your faith that determines whether this remains a theory for you, whether you keep operating like mere men or move to the realm of the sons of God. Many people believe in Jesus and all He has done, but for some reason, they cannot see that this includes them also. They believe when they see the works of God in other people's lives, and they will believe the minister, but simply cannot see themselves living in that realm. I want to tell you today that all that Jesus did was for you. From today, when you read the Bible, put your name in the place of the apostles; see yourself in the scriptures. I love the scripture that says: As it is written about me in the Scriptures (Psalms 40:7 NLT).

All these rights have your name attached to them; this 'God life' is for you too. Stop detaching yourself from the blessed life that God has sacrificed so much for you to live. I am amazed when I see Christians who believe God can heal but somehow don't believe God can do it for them, or that God can change someone's story but won't believe that God can do it for them. Somewhere and somehow, the enemy has deceived many to think that they are exempt and the little is their portion. This is where we get sayings like "this is my portion" or "God didn't intend it for all." Please, can someone show me where they find this in the scriptures? I can confidently tell you that the Bible says that God shows no partiality (Acts 10:34). Romans 2:11 reaffirms this truth: For there is no partiality with God. And there we have it, by the mouth of two or three witnesses every word may be established (Matthew 18:16). Believers need to stop using poor examples as doctrines because we do not know the circumstances that caused the individual not to experience God's best. Instead, we must rest on what God has set as an example repeatedly throughout the scriptures. For example, every time God was with a person, they were blessed, they had victory, and they operated in dominion. All these good things were proof that God was in the picture. Throughout the Bible, it was only when God was absent or displeased that we saw bondage, suffering and all sorts of evil. That tells me that suffering is not God's intention for you and me.

CHAPTER 3

The Mystery of Faith to the Believer

Because it has been given to you to know the mystery of the kingdom of heaven…

Matthew 13:11

Many believers have misunderstood faith and limited its effectiveness in their lives. For many, faith is simply a wish list, which means if they concentrate really hard, they may be able to zap whatever they desire into existence. So, when we look at the lives of many believers across the world, we see a pattern of inconsistency when it relates to the power their faith produces; today they receive their testimonies and tomorrow they don't. However, for a believer, our faith must have a stable foundation that remains sure in our lives. Everything we are is based on our faith; hence we are called believers. The power of the cross, the power of resurrection and all that salvation has to offer, all rest on the foundation of our faith.

The Bible tells us in Psalms 11:3 that if the foundations are destroyed, what can the righteous do? While the CEB version says what can a righteous person possibly accomplish? We need to understand that the devil's strategy is always to mess with our foundation or our source because that is the root of unlocking our power. This leads me to understand that the devil is not our greatest weakness, but it is our ignorance and lack of knowledge of the truth that makes many fall short.

> You shall know the truth (the mystery), and that
> truth shall make you free
>
> John 8:32 (paraphrased)

What is faith?

To answer this, we will start with John 19:30:

> So when Jesus had received the sour wine, He
> said, "It is finished!" And bowing His head, He
> gave up His spirit.

Therefore He says:

> When He ascended on high, He led captivity captive, and gave gifts to men." (Now this, "He ascended"—what does it mean but that He also first descended into the lower parts of the earth? He who descended is also the One who ascended far above all the heavens that He might fill all things.) And He Himself gave some to be apostles, some prophets, some evangelists, and some pastors and teachers, for the equipping of the saints for the work of ministry, for the edifying of the body of Christ, till we all come to the unity of the faith and of the knowledge of the Son of God, to a perfect man, to the measure of the stature of the fullness of Christ

Ephesians 4:8-13).

The faith mentioned in Ephesians speaks of the Kingdom of God (a new constitution and way of life that governs you and me). The perfect man mentioned in verse 13 speaks of the type of life and blessing that now has been allocated to you as a child of God. Remember that throughout scriptures, God has been obsessed with giving us a future and a hope (Jeremiah 29:11) and the promise, that by faith in Jesus Christ, might be given to those who believe (Galatians 3:22-23). The power of your faith, therefore, lies in the discovery of God's Kingdom and the Kingdom's ruler. It is paramount that you understand that faith has nothing to do with your desires or hoping that they will be granted.

God is not committed to giving you anything that He did not agree to and He will not prosper you where He has not sent you. If He does not send you, neither He nor His resources are permitted to be there with you: without me you can do nothing (John 15:5). However, when He sends you, you will lack nothing: Jesus asked His disciples, when I sent you, did you lack anything? (Luke 22:35).

You must make it your priority to discover what your portion is, what your inheritance is and what His will is for you. It is your enforcement of that in your life that is faith. I believe God can do what He said He would do and I trust that He is faithful to stick to His words.

> By faith Sarah herself also received strength to conceive seed, and she bore a child when she was past the age, because she judged Him faithful who had promised.
>
> Hebrew 11:11

It is your faith that births and forms your actions. Some people have, for many years without results, been focused on trying to prove their faith by their actions. They will do all sorts in the name of faith, only to be frustrated. Your efforts mean nothing if you don't believe, but if you act because you have believed in what He has said, you will have it.

I remember when I was about to have my first child and I allowed anxiety to overwhelm me during the last period of my pregnancy. I was so frustrated at being pregnant that I was willing to do anything to get the baby out. I took on everyone's advice on speeding up the delivery of my son, and so I started exercising excessively. By the time I was to have the baby, I was worn out and had to have a C-section.

At this point, I realised I had put everything in my own hands even though I professed to have faith. I quickly went back to God, and I asked Him to take over, and He spoke a word to me, "With long life will I satisfy you." (Psalm 91:16). I had always had a fear of surgery, but when I heard those words, I knew with all my heart that I was going to be okay because I believed Him. Anything I have ever received from God was merely because I believed the words He spoke to me and ran with it. It shows in my actions. It's not my job to know all the details, but it is my job to move because He said so. Realise that faith takes the focus away from you and puts it on God; on what He said and what He can do. Faith has nothing to do with you.

The Word of God

You must learn to run to the Word of God first to discover what your expectation, mindset and opinion should be on any matter. Many people react to situations in their lives without going to the Bible to learn God's take on the subject. Only for them to find out that their reaction is the total opposite of God's Word.

Anytime I disagreed with my husband's choices concerning our home; I reacted in a way that made him uneasy. If I felt that his decision was the wrong one, I would nag at him until he changed his mind. I didn't understand why my behaviour made him uncomfortable because I wasn't rude. I only forced the matter for the sake of my family's welfare.

However, one day the Holy Spirit whisper in my ear, "You are not the one responsible for the family, he is, and you are his helper." Suddenly it hit me; I was busy doing someone else's job in my marriage. God's expectation for me as a wife is specific, and I would only please God, and our union would be blessed only if I operate according to God's design. I was reacting to a situation in a manner that was the complete opposite to that which God expected of me. Therefore I could not reap His support in the matter. God's expectation for me as a wife is to be the help he needs to get it right. Therefore, I support him in prayer and create a conducive environment to ensure that he is always hearing from God. However, my place is not to make the final decision because I am not responsible for it.

I looked at the scriptures and saw how Sarah obeyed her husband. She followed him down to Egypt and even obeyed his instruction to lie. Her obedience forced God to step in and rescue them both. Don't get me wrong, yes I can share my views, and yes my views should be considered because I am his equal partner. In no way, shape or form am I suggesting that a woman should be trampled on and disregarded in her home. However, if your help is not needed, you cannot force it. Advice is just that: advice. Even if you are right, it is up to the person seeking it to decide whether or not to follow it.

When you decide to position yourself according to God's Word, you can enforce your rights, and you have the full support of heaven to ensure that those rights are your experience. The Word of God is the settled conclusion. Forever O Lord, Your word is settled in heaven (Psalm 119:89). For example, if you discover the Word of the Lord that says the earth is the Lord's and all its fullness (Psalm 24:1), for every beast of the forest is Mine and the cattle on a thousand hills (Psalms 50:10), and that we are children of God, and if children, then heirs – heirs of God (Romans 8:16).

Nothing resembling poverty will be around you because you will not tolerate it. The devil can play with your emotions, but once you know the truth, you can reject any counterfeit. Saying "I am a believer, God I believe the integrity of your Word, and this is not of God, so Satan, I rebuke you in the name and authority of Jesus Christ." All the enemy wants to do is see whether or not you believe what you say you believe.

Many of us say we believe things, but when circumstances come our way, we shift from what we say we believe. If that is all it takes to alter your beliefs, the enemy will keep throwing temptations your way, knowing it is enough to get you to walk out of what God has in store for you. Stand firm on what you believe until you see it manifest in your life.

CHAPTER 4

The Foundation of Relationship

My sheep hear My voice; I know them,
and they follow Me

John 10:27

Everything we have learned so far is on the platform of your relationship with God and Jesus Christ. Faith will only produce to the extent that you believe God, but how can you believe someone you do not know? You don't know their character or their personality. You don't even know what they are and their capability.

I have been with my husband now for a lengthy period. In that period, we have gained a stronger knowledge of what each other's strengths and weaknesses are. As we have fellowshipped over the years, I have come to know what he can and can't do. I remember one day he came home laughing because someone had told him I did something. Nodding his head, he said, "I would wish it wasn't true, but I know my wife too well to know that she is fully capable of such."

That is what a relationship does. It gives you an insight into the capacity of the one with whom you are in a relationship. Many would love to believe everything that we have previously spoken about. It is exciting to hear that there is such a great inheritance in God. But the only hindrance is that there is no history between them and God, so the devil keeps short-changing them with a life less than the one they are supposed to be living.

Some believe that it is fate that causes us to have fortune or misfortune. However, a relationship with God will tell you otherwise. God does not have it in Him to desire lack, sickness or anything short of the experience He has for you. When the enemy wants to bring something your way and wants you to accept it as God's will for you, a personal relationship will tell you that God can't do that to you; it is just not in Him.

The Power of History

There have been many times when my belief in God has been challenged. The struggle that you are going through seems more real than anything else, even any belief that you may have. At that present time, you sometimes don't feel like you even

31

know what you believe. All you know that is the frustration of the current situation is overwhelming you, and that is what is real. This is the point where many of us start asking God the famous question, "Why me?" or we ask ourselves, "If God is real, then why…". I recall when I had an, 'if God was real' moment. Despite the question in my head, my heart remembered my history. In those moments, I compared the seasons in my life when I was intimate with God, and I made Him my everything to those when I was distant from Him. My distance from God always brought emptiness to my world, even when things appeared to be going well for me. However, whenever I stayed close to Him, even in spite of many challenges, there was an assurance that He would work it out for me. The end always confirms it.

Just taking a moment to reason with my heart dispels any doubt of God's presence and willingness in my life. Nothing could convince me of God and His heart towards me more than my history with God. Anytime my head questions the present, my heart remembers the past and gives me such great hope for my tomorrow. It is so important to cherish your journey with God and to remember what He has done for you. This confirms what He will do for you. I will say this, anything that has ever gone wrong in my life has been because of my shortcomings, not God's. God will never tempt you, but He will use every situation to take you to a beautiful place of glory, peace, and joy. And in it all, God will be glorified.

I am a great believer that for every Christian, the childbirth process is a stress-free one and that every believer is exempt from the pain and suffering that is commonly associated with the childbirth process. It is your right. Why? Christ has redeemed us from the curse of the law (Galatians 3:13). However, with this belief, I still had an entirely different experience when it came to my own childbirth experience. Many would ask, "Where is God in all of this?" Few people would be honest enough to say that He was right there ready to keep His side of the deal, but they messed up.

During my first pregnancy, like most women, I was so frustrated towards the end that I allowed anxiety to take full control of me. The pregnancy itself was glorious; even when the doctor wanted to find something wrong, there was nothing to be found. I just had had enough of being pregnant and was willing to do anything to get the baby out. I also remember looking at my friends, who were pregnant, giving birth two to three weeks early. My mind and my heart were everywhere except resting in God and His plan. Instead, I took the wheel and decided that the baby would come when I decided. By the time the baby was ready to come, I was emotionally exhausted, and I wanted a

C-section. All I remembered doing was asking for forgiveness at that moment and immediately I felt God take over the situation. Right then I had an assurance that my baby and I were going to be just fine. I rested. God never messes up. We cannot blame God for the choices we make, but we can ask Him to step in and take the wheel.

Building and sustaining a relationship with God

If this personal journey between you and God is so important, how can you build one or maintain the one you've started? The first key is to spend time getting to know God. Many Christians have had this shoved down their throats; how vital it is to spend time with God, to have prayer time, devotional and so on. A wise man once said, "When the purpose of a thing is not known, abuse is inevitable." This is why many believers struggle with spending time with Jesus. A devotional to them is nothing more than a routine that validates their Christianity.

I remember the moment I decided to make Jesus Lord of my life. I was raised in a Christian family, so I always believed in God; I just wasn't ready to live a life God approved of until one New Year's Eve service. My colleague invited me to a church, and my mother had insisted that I follow the family tradition of spending New Year's Eve at church. Since I wasn't interested in going to my mother's church, I took my colleague up on her offer to visit her church. However, upon arrival, the queue for church was longer than that of a club. After the struggle to get into the building, the usher took me to the overflow to watch a screen. Disinterested, I walked out only to return and be sent to the overflow in the tent by the freezing river. After his message, the pastor called for anyone who wanted God to rededicate their life. Sobbing uncontrollably, I practically crawled to the front, and I decided to make Jesus the Lord of my life. This moment, however, seemed all too familiar. The music would cease, the service would finish, and the next day I would find myself in the arms of the person I vowed never to see again.

So when the music faded, and the atmosphere returned to normal, I knelt by the side of my bed and said to God, "I want this to be real, so now what? I don't do rules and all Christianity is about is keeping rules." For the first time, I heard the voice of God speak to me, and He said, "Just love me." Those words kept ringing in my heart for days.

Then I thought to myself, how do I love someone that I don't know? Immediately I had a passion for reading the Bible. I needed to know this God; I needed to find out who He was. You cannot build a relationship with God outside of His Word, the Bible. It is the Bible that is our first reference point. It tells us who He is and His mind is concerning us. It is the words from the Bible that the Holy Spirit uses to recommunicate a message to us in our current situation. The Bible is the voice of God to you. A believer that does not spend time with God and allow Him to communicate His thoughts for them is a believer that will be deceived out of receiving the best of God for their life.

Spending time with the Word isn't sufficient. You must learn to spend time in environments that will encourage growth in your relationship with God. Some so many people want a close relationship with God but are around 'sometime-ish' Christians. I think a Christian who isn't sold out to God is more damaging to your walk with God than even an unbeliever. When you are around a non-Christian, the truth is that you are wary of their lifestyle because you know that they don't believe what you believe. Naturally, you will be careful not to copy their way of life. But when you are dear friends with people who claim to be Christians but live opposite to The Faith, you lower your guard and end up imitating them because you think you are of the same mindset.

Many years ago, God spoke to me and said, "If you are going to fall, it will be in my house." That shocked me, but then I realised it was very accurate. Does your environment push you to want more of God or to become complacent in God? Are you growing spiritually or have you lost the passion that once was? Check your environment. Check the people that you are around, check what is entering your soul through your eyes and your ears.

Don't sacrifice your relationship with God through your daily choices. This doesn't mean that the solution is isolation because that too can lead to stagnation in your walk with God. Separation from other believers will make you believe that the state of your Christian walk is perfect, whereas surrounding yourself with fervent Christians will force you to grow in God.

> Let us not neglect our meeting together, as some people do
>
> Hebrews 10:25 (NLT).

Anything or any place that does not contribute to the continued health of my marriage is intolerable to me because my marriage and my relationship with Samuel are of the utmost importance. This is the same approach with my relationship with God. I cannot afford to lose my relationship with God because then I lose everything. If I lose God what would be the point of my existence? There are so many Christians who place no value on their relationship with God. Therefore, they sacrifice it daily without realising it.

CHAPTER 5

Riches

The earth is the Lord's, and all its fullness,
the world and those who dwell therein.

Psalm 24:1

The matter of wealth has been controversial for believers worldwide for centuries. It is a topic that has brought many to a place of confusion. Many are torn between a desire to be financially free and the desire to be spiritual. Whenever confusion arises in life, my solution is to return to God's Word and let its guiding light teach me what God's mindset is towards the matter.

The truth is that it does not matter what people's opinions are or what their conclusions are because you are only to live your life according to the standard of God. It is just God's opinion that matters because you are accountable to Him alone. I can think a lot of things, but what I think doesn't matter because the view of the One who created the universe trumps mine any day.

People give so much reverence to the opinions of people that cannot improve their own lives, yet they ignore God, who not only wants to provide them with an incredible life but also can do just that. I always like to inform people that not everything that sounds spiritual is spiritual, especially when it is unscriptural.

Every spiritual thing has its foundation in the scriptures. It is by this simple truth that we judge everything to know what is right and what is not. I am yet to see the person who can, from the depths of their heart, tell me that poverty is good. Poverty leads many to sin. No one living in lack enjoys it; they might learn to survive in it, but they don't enjoy it. That's why when a route of escape is given to anyone in need; they snatch it with everything inside of them.

Imagine having kids and having no means to provide for them. This isn't even a matter of having your desires for luxury fulfilled, but just your needs met. On what basis can someone say that riches are not God's desire?

What God doesn't desire for us is to be ruled by riches and material things. When material things rule a person, they don't trust God to provide for their needs and therefore hold onto what they have to provide for themselves. Another reason God doesn't want material things to rule us is that many connect their worth to the things they have and that is very wrong. Nothing you own determines your worth or your identity; that is only found in God through Jesus.

Yes, God doesn't want money to rule us, but that doesn't mean that He doesn't want us to have money or wealth. The truth is that God wants us to have in abundance so that He can use us to bless and influence the world around us. Do you know why the world listens to those in Hollywood with corrupt and evil mindsets? Because they have enough money to give to causes to make a difference. Imagine if those giving the most significant sums to causes across the nations of the world and making a difference with their wealth were believers. The world would have no choice but to respect and even follow our way of life. Look at this scripture in Ecclesiastes 9:16:

> Wisdom is better than strength. Nevertheless, the poor man's wisdom is despised, and his words are not heard.

The answers to the crises in the world today are inside the believer, but until we start walking in the riches Christ has laid out for us, the world will not be willing to listen to us. Let me explain God's mind concerning financial prosperity for you. The Bible says that the earth is the Lord's and everything inside it (Psalm 24:1). How then can God live in an abundance of wealth and rejoice in the lack of His children? That doesn't add up. On the contrary, God is saddened when we don't have. It is His passion not just to meet our needs, but to give us abundance (John 10:10).

Why is it so difficult to believe that God wants to be kind to you? This is the same God that asks you to be kind to one another. Surely He wouldn't ask of you something He himself isn't capable of? We know He wouldn't because the Bible tells us that He wants us to imitate Him and that He is a just and righteous God.

God is desperate for you to have the best. He created the best for you because He has access to the best. The Bible says that we are joint heirs with Christ Jesus. What exactly does that mean?

It means that everything that Christ has access to is yours and not just finances. The entire world is available to meet your needs. Everything is set for your benefit and your good. Here's what the Bible says:

And we know that all things work together for
good to those who love God, to those who are
the called according to His purpose.

Romans 8:28

If God owns it, then you have a right to it. At no point in
Jesus' life did He experience lack. The simple fact that Judas
was needed as a treasurer shows the level of wealth to which
Jesus had access. Even when He needed it, the earth brought
forth money.

Nevertheless, lest we offend them, go to the sea,
cast in a hook, and take the fish that comes up
first. And when you have opened its mouth, you
will find a piece of money; take that and give it to
them for Me and you.

Matthew 17:27

This truth has filled me with so much confidence that regardless of my current position, I know that all the resources
in the earth are available to me. When God talks about giving
you riches, He is not simply talking about finances; He is talking
about resources. When you know that you have the right to
resources, you know that wherever you are and whatever you

need, you have the right to have it.

So no matter how difficult or farfetched it may seem, as long as it is required you can have it. I remember when I embarked on the idea of opening a clothing store. I was only a young graduate, and I did not come from a 'silver spoon' background. I had this great idea, but the reality of the finances in my bank account did not tally up with my dream.

I remember going to several banks to get a loan, as that seemed like the reasonable thing to do, only to be rejected by every single one of them. It looked like I had just two options: I could carry out my vision on a much smaller scale (which is wise in some instances); or I could lay the whole idea to rest and call it a day. Then the scripture hit me, the earth is the Lord's and everything inside it. Well, I thought to myself, my earthly mother would give me everything I needed if she could. How much more my heavenly Father? If He genuinely owned the entire earth, then a couple of tens of thousands of pounds wasn't too much for Him to give me.

> Ask, and it will be given to you; seek, and you
> will find; knock, and it will be opened to you. For
> everyone who asks receives, and he who seeks
> finds, and to him who knocks it will be opened.
> Or what man is there among you who, if his son

asks for bread, will give him a stone? Or if he asks for a fish, will he give him a serpent? If you then, being evil, know how to give good gifts to your children, how much more will your Father who is in heaven give good things to those who ask Him!

Matthew 7:7-11

So I asked, and I asked believing that it was possible. How? I knew with everything inside of me that God could and that He would because He delighted in it. The story ended with me opening up the store without having to downsize my vision and without a loan. God opened up the hands in which He had put my resources and connected me to them.

When it comes to the aspect of wealth, many of us struggle through life because we don't know it is our right and that it gives God pleasure. For this reason, we don't ask for big things, and if we are coerced into asking, we don't believe. And if we don't believe, it is guaranteed that we will not receive.

Have you seen an heir to the throne live in poverty, lack or want? No matter the state of the economy, the Queen is always arrayed in wealth and so are her family. I remember one of the princesses wearing a wardrobe worth £35,000; meanwhile, the country was debating the increasing rate of poverty in the nation. This is where many get confused. How can I be in wealth while others are in poverty? The Bible says:

> So I said, "Wisdom is better than strength." Nevertheless, the poor man's wisdom is despised, and his words are not heard. Ecclesiastes 9:16

Though you may have a heart for people in need, it is wealth that allows you to relieve the pain of the needy. What good are your words, when your hands cannot do anything about it? So God blessed Abraham, and his blessing enabled him to be a blessing to generations. You cannot give what you don't have. Do not have to feel bad for belonging to royalty, but instead embrace it and use it for the benefit of others also.

The challenge is that many are ruled by the desire to be rich and to have wealth for selfish gains. So much so that they begin to have a love for money, which the Bible says is the root of all evil. Money itself is not evil, but the love of it is. The moment money starts ruling you, you have no morals, no values or principles and would do anything just to get it. You are no longer satisfied with receiving from God and would do anything to get rich.

Many lie for wealth and do things that they know God is not pleased with. The problem is that when we try to obtain wealth by living life the way we perceive He isn't proud of, we end up hiding from God and the ends of such stories are not great. So people conclude, "See, it is not a righteous thing for you to have wealth." No! It is not a righteous thing for you to have wealth by means that are against God and what He stands for. Why then are so many believers in lack and want? The devil's main priority is to move believers far away from all that God has laid aside for you. He will, therefore, take great delight in keeping you in lack and want.

Think about it: you want to spread the good news of the Gospel to certain people, but they know that if you could swap your lives with theirs, you would and simply because they have and you don't. This is why I get frustrated when people complain about wealthy ministers but don't complain about the fact that the heads of worldly organisations are lavishly wealthy. We want to find some normality in living without while the world lives with all that is our Father's. There is no logic in that whatsoever. It is even entirely against scriptures. Throughout scriptures, the proof that God was with someone was that they became financially blessed amongst other things: The man became rich, and his wealth continued to grow until he became very wealthy. He had so many flocks and herds and servants that the Philistines envied him. (Genesis 26:13-14)

We are to be the envy of the world; to show the world the nature of God including His great wealth. A wealth that has no end. Stop embracing a life of struggle. This is not your identity as a believer. Get tired of the devil stealing from you and walk into all that is yours in Jesus Christ.

CHAPTER 6

Power

And Jesus came and spoke to them, saying, "All authority has
been given to Me in heaven and on earth."

Matthew 28:18

When we talk about the believer having power,
many do not know what that looks like in reality.
It seems like an elusive concept while the ability
to exercise power attributed to you in Christ Jesus remains dormant. The main reason for this chapter is to give you a clear
understanding of what power should mean for every believer
on a daily basis.

I want to start by making this definite link. The Bible says
that Christ has all possible authority in heaven and on earth.
The same Bible also says that you are joint heirs with Christ
Jesus (Romans 8:17). Therefore, you now have all authority in
heaven and on earth. The Bible goes on to further reinforce this
truth for you and me in Matthew 18:18:

Assuredly, I say to you, whatever you bind on
earth will be bound in heaven, and whatever you
loose on earth will be loosed in heaven.

Therefore, you have power! To utilise this God-given gift, you need to understand what it means to have power. In its purest definition, power is the ability to do; it is the ability to cause something to happen or not to happen. The ability to alter the course of a thing or enforce an outcome. When God said you now have power, He was saying that you now can implement particular outcomes in your life and the lives of those around you.

For example, we see that in Mark 4:39, Jesus had authority over the weather and spoke to it and the outcome that He desired was what was manifested. The Spirit of God illuminated this scripture in my heart one day. I was driving down from an appointment and rain fell heavily from the skies. There was no way that anyone would want to be caught in such weather. The ministry had a conference the next day, and the forecast was that it was going rain heavily again.

Well, I didn't want to experience that, and this scripture was brought to my heart by the Spirit of God. I pointed to the skies, and I spoke to it in the name of Jesus. I spoke to it with the full assurance that God said I had the power and authority to do so. Obviously, the devil threw thoughts my way to make me withdraw my declaration of faith and stop me experiencing the manifestation of what I had declared: "God won't answer prayer on the weather, what about others that need the rain?" "If people only come to a conference because of the weather then they are not strong Christians." These contrary thoughts rushed through my mind, but I refused to entertain them. I opened my mouth again and vocalised my desire. It did not matter what anyone else desired from God, all I knew was that I did not want it to rain and the Bible told me that I had authority over the weather. I drove home parked in the rain and struggled into the house soaking.

The next morning I woke up to the pitter patter of the rain. The first thought was, "well God doesn't need the sun for you to have a great conference, and whoever needs to come will come." But that scripture shot up in my heart once again and I received full assurance that I did have authority over the weather regardless of how it appeared. I spoke to the weather and then began to prepare myself and the kids for the day ahead. As God would have it, the manifestation of my declaration came through. Despite the weather report and the sight of rain, all rain dried up. I went to the conference dry, we had a glorious time and I came home dry.

The Life God Has For You

The truth is that if we do not seize the opportunity to put into practice what we have read in the Word of God, we may never experience the life that God has set up for us to live as His children. His promises towards us as Christians aren't fairy tales or slogans that make us tingle with excitement; they are the reality of the truth we have access to. You have to have the mentality that if the Bible says, then undoubtedly we must experience it. Stop being satisfied with the sayings and slogans and push for the power of your salvation.

Never be satisfied with less when God wants you to have more. Life isn't fair, so if you just sit back and go through life, you will end up with a lot less than what you are entitled to. God has set up a particular life for you, and you can create your outcomes and surroundings. Understand this; God has put you in charge of the outcome of your life.

You must understand that inside you is the ability to bring about life or death, to enforce growth and progress or to suffer in lack and want. Whatever happens around you or in your life is based on nothing but what you have allowed by the authority that Christ has given you. When you own a home and pay your electric bill, the energy supplier has given you the power to determine whether the house should be in darkness or light. You can exercise your right to light and comfort by switching

Mimi Ajala

on your light, or you can stumble and struggle in the dark even though you can bring about light. The choice there is yours. The same truth that applies to us as believers.

How to enforce your authority

The first thing is that you have to be fully persuaded that God means it when He says you have all authority in heaven and on earth. If you don't believe that you have this authority, then there is no way you will be confident to exercise it. It is this belief in their delegated authority that allows police officers to walk up to a person and boldly declare them arrested. Imagine a police officer that did not believe he had such a right. That officer would witness a crime and stand by not considering it was in their capacity to do anything about the situation. Instead, that officer would wait for help when help was inside them.

Many Christians around the globe are looking for help and being pitied when they are the helper. Why? Because they have not been fully persuaded that they can change the course of a situation and enforce the desired outcome in the authority that Christ has given them. Belief always breeds confidence and confidence drives one to action.

The second is that you must exercise your authority by your speech.

52

The Life God Has For You

The tongue has the POWER of life and death

Proverbs 18:21 (NIV)

It is incredible that believers speak as the world speaks. For this reason, they suffer as the world suffers. This is not meant to be so. Rather than professing negatives with your mouth, make a conscious effort to declare and therefore enforce what God has willed to do for you in every circumstance. Ask yourself, what is God's desire for this situation, and then you speak that. Now be careful that you don't assume God's desire; make sure that it is derived from the Word of God.

Some people say the most unscriptural things just because it sounds spiritual. I remember having a conversation with someone. I had just finished praying for the restoration of someone's health and they asked me how do I know that it's not God's will that this person dies? They explained that God was sovereign and as unpleasant as it could be, God could take someone's life like that.

Now my husband has emphatically taught me to find my backing for any belief in the Word of God. Knowing this, I searched the scriptures within me. What this person said sounded spiritual. However, the Bible says:

1. He will take away sickness and disease from me: Deuteronomy 7:15

2. He will restore my health: Jeremiah 30:17

3. He wishes above all things that I am in good health: 3 John 2

Well, from that I knew immediately that God could not be pleased in the passing away of a believer through sickness. That is not the way we sleep in the Lord.

I cannot overemphasise how important it is for you as a child of God to know the Word of God. It is essential that you fill yourself with the Word, not just sermons but also reading the Bible itself. How can you know when something is contrary to God's will for you when you don't know what is in the Bible and what is not? It's impossible!

We have Christians all over the world that do not open their Bibles, so they are living far below the standard that God intends for them to live. Please make it a priority to read your Bible. The problem is that because many don't understand the purpose of picking up the Bible, they quickly find it tedious. For some, it is only a religious act that Christians do. This is far from the truth. The Bible says in Proverbs 4:20-21 (NIV):

My son pay attention to what I say; turn your ear
to my words. Do not let them out of your sight,
keep them within your heart; for they are life to
those who find them and health to one's whole
body.

It is your closeness with the Word of God that keeps you continuously living the God life. When you know within your heart of what God wants, you can say no to the devil's cheap counterfeit offers for your life. Let's quickly look at the story of the woman with the issue of blood in Luke 8:43-48:

Now a woman, having a flow of blood for twelve years, who
had spent all her livelihood on physicians and could not be
healed by any, came from behind and touched the border of
His garment. And immediately her flow of blood stopped.
And Jesus said, "Who touched Me?" When all denied it, Peter
and those with him[a] said, "Master, the multitudes throng
and press You, and You say, 'Who touched Me?'" But Jesus
said, "Somebody touched Me, for I perceived power going
out from Me." Now when the woman saw that she was not
hidden, she came trembling; and falling down before Him, she
declared to Him in the presence of all the people the reason
she had touched Him and how she was healed immediately.
And He said to her, "Daughter, be of good cheer;[c] your faith
has made you well. Go in peace.

Now, look at verse 44. What could have inspired this woman's action? What was on the border of his garment? Everyone was pushing up on Jesus and engaging in the hype that would have followed this phenomenon. Most of them were suffering in their situations with the solution right in front of them, yet excited by hype only.

That mirrors so many believers in the world today. Every Sunday they go to Church, they are a part of the community of believers, yet have not connected to the power available to this community. But where this woman was concerned, her action was able to release power for her situation. How?

> But for you who fear My name, the Sun of Righteousness shall arise with healing in His wings;
> And you shall go out and grow fat stall-fed calves.
>
> Malachi 4:2

The hem (border) of a man's clothes then could also be referred to as wings. So this woman probably had a revelation from the scripture to which she could apply her faith, and because her faith was based on the Word of God, God had to honour it. Her action had purpose based on God's word, which enabled access to power.

God will not answer any prayer that is outside the boundaries of His will. You may desperately want Him to grant your request, but unless it is based on His will, there is no guarantee of an answer. Hear James 4:3:

> When you ask, you do not receive, because you
> ask with wrong motives, that you may spend
> what you get on your pleasures.

How can you be sure that what you believe God for is His will, if you don't read His Word? Don't be so concerned about how to read the Bible; be concerned with the fact that you need to read the Bible. Come up with what suits you best and be realistic. This doesn't benefit anyone other than you, so you don't have to prove anything. Settle down with yourself and analyse your life but don't go a day without reading the Word.

I have three kids all under the age of 5, I am a wife, and I run a ministry. Early on in my pregnancy with my last child, I was also working full time as the Head of UK sales for a FTSE 100 company. It was crucial for me to use the time God has given me each day effectively. I have a routine that works for me. In the morning, I wake up, and before I move anywhere, I pray. I need the Holy Spirit involved in the day I am about to head into, and I need to show my appreciation to God for giving me another opportunity to live. Then I use a devotional to get me to meditate on one verse through the Word. It's not intense, but it is heartfelt. Throughout the day, I meditate on the Word, and I pray. I don't separate myself to do this; it is simply a part of me. So I may be dealing with some work or my family, but if I am not in a conversation, I will be praying and talking to God or meditating on a message or scripture. I tend to have a routine with my family, which means that my kids are in bed at a particular time, then I spend some time with my husband or relaxing. After this, before I go to bed, I open up my Bible and intensely read it. I make a point that I don't go to the Word when I am tired and ready to sleep. I must still have energy in me. I usually study one book of the Bible at a time, so I stay on that book until I have finished. I don't mean that I finish the entire book in one sitting. There are many ways to study. For example, some people do character studies.

Now that is what works for me. When I was younger, I would do my intense Word study in the morning because I had no demands on my time, no kids to get ready and no work to go to, etc. The point is that God is not interested in how you get the Word into you, but he does care that you get it into you. It is not a religious activity, but it is a necessity to keep you living the life that God has intended for you.

CHAPTER 7

Blessing

Behold, I have received a command to bless; He has blessed, **and I cannot reverse** it.

Numbers 23:20

We often use the term "I am blessed" but do we truly know what it means? When you say you are blessed, do you live by the revelation and power of that truth? Yes, it is correct that you are blessed, but today I pray that the Lord opens your spiritual eyes to the truth and power of that statement as you read this book.

The first time we encounter God blessing people in the Bible is in the book of Genesis 1:28:

Then God blessed them, and God said to them, "Be fruitful and multiply; fill the earth and subdue it; have dominion over…"

We see it again when God speaks to Abraham in Genesis 12:2:

I will make you a great nation; I will bless
you, And make your name great; And you shall
be a blessing.

So, what does God mean when He says that we are blessed? The blessing is the empowerment and force that enables
you to live in the inheritance and dominion God has given to
you. When you say you are blessed, you are acknowledging the
power that God has spoken into existence on the earth to make
things work on your behalf.

There are people on the earth that because of the blessing
of the Lord upon their lives, have things working in their fa-
vour. They don't appear to be the brightest, but when it's time
for a promotion they are noticed. As a believer and a child of
God, you have a force working for you on the earth that cannot
be resisted by anyone or anything. That force is the blessing of
God on your life.

You know the scripture in Romans 8:28 says all things work
together for good to those who love God. It is the force of the
blessing of God that makes all things work together for you. If
you don't understand this truth, you will spend your days trying to do things by your strength with no fruits to show for it.
You are blessed and empowered by God. The blessing of God

is a force that will drive you to the top of the earth; to your high places. The empowerment of God (blessing) on your life is a force that repels the low places of the earth. Have you not wondered why are dissatisfied with mediocrity and failure? It is because the blessing of God on you is pushing you away from where God has not designed you for and towards where God desires you to be.

Every blessing of God sets the believer in the place of dominion. The blessing of God sets you over things, not under them. You are blessed! When you say you are blessed, it means that you have now been empowered by God Himself. Now, how can God empower you? How can you have the force of God working on your behalf and be defeated by any challenge of the earth?

David was so aware of the fact that He was blessed that He faced Goliath confidently. Most of us know that story very well. What was the difference between David and the rest of the Israelites? The same force working for David was equal to the force working in every single Israelite. Nothing can resist that power. The Bible says that the sea saw that force and its only option was to flee (Psalm 114:3). Any Israelite could have defeated Goliath, but only one (David) was conscious of that blessing. This empowered him above everything, including

Goliath, as he put that force to work. Don't live life in ignorance of the truth that you are blessed of God and don't allow the blessing of God to be dormant in your life. The force that is not put to work will not work for you.

CHAPTER 8

Honour

Their nobles shall be from among them, And their governor shall come from their midst; Then I will cause him to draw near, And he shall approach Me; For who is this who pledged his heart to approach Me?' says the Lord.

Jeremiah 30:21

The dictionary definition of honour is to be given high respect and great esteem. The world does not have to like you, but God is setting you up in such a way that they will not be able to deny you the great respect that Jesus has purchased for you by His blood. I love it that the Bible says in Revelations 5 that Jesus died to receive for you and me, not just respect, but honour, which means high respect.

Please understand that you are honourable by the blood of the Lord; there is now a high esteem attributed to you, and you must carry yourself as such. Many of us comport ourselves as people who have no honour, which no one should value or respect because we do not see much in ourselves. Inside you is the capacity to influence the course of your environment and your world.

The church has so lost its place in the world because we do not walk in the honour that has been bestowed on us. In the times of old, a country could not plan without consulting the head of the Church. Now the world makes decisions and forces believers to follow because we refuse to walk in the honour assigned to us. I believe with all my heart that God is restoring the Church (every believer in Christ) to its honourable position. My prayer for you is that you are among the Church as she is restored to her intended place of honour. What does that mean for you? Jeremiah 30:21 says the noble of the land (the influential people of the country, the earth and its organisations and institutions) will come from among the children of God.

Whatever institution you are in, God will make you a significant person. This means that we need to be aiming for positions of influence. Why is it that when you look at the management of an organisation, you do not see a believer? If you don't understand that you must be in a position of honour, then even when opportunities arise, you won't apply for them. Why can't a believer be the CEO of the corporation they are working in? Why can't the government be filled with Christians? We complain that the laws made are evil, but we refuse to become the lawmakers. As long as we have a job meeting our basic needs, then we are satisfied. This mindset is so wrong that I believe it is sinful because we become the obstacle to God changing the world. God will only change the world through His children, but if His children have no influence what change can they bring about? For the sake of the gospel and the sake of the work of God in our generation, we must rise to the place of honour.

Imagine if the Prime Minister of the UK or the Head of State of your nation were from the Church. Imagine if believers owned the largest companies. There would be a revival. Have you ever noticed that the majority of the people in the Bible that we look up to were taught the works of God and elevated to positions of influence?

- Joseph was the Prime Minister

- Moses was in Pharaoh's house

- Daniel was a Prime Minister

- David was the King

- Jesus started a movement that could not be denied

- The apostles were noticed by the rulers of the land even though they did not like them.

Mimi Ajala

They don't have to like you, but they have to honour you.
However, you must first believe that you are honourable. You
are not for the low places of the earth. Reject that notion with
everything in you. It is your season for elevation and God will
lift you to the position of honour in Jesus name.

CHAPTER 9

Glory

But we all, with unveiled face, beholding as in a mirror the glory of the Lord, are being transformed into the same image from glory to glory, just as by the Spirit of the Lord.

2 Corinthians 3:18

God is desperate for us to live in His glory. This is a massive part of the fruit and joy of your salvation. Jesus, while on the earth, was the image of God's glory. Some of you may be asking, what exactly is God's glory?

It is everything about God that makes us say, "Wow." It causes us to stand in awe of him. God's glory is what makes Him indescribable. If you saw Jesus then you saw God; you saw God's capacity and beauty in the life of Jesus. This is how it is supposed to be for every child of God on the face of the planet. People are supposed to see you and be in awe of you. They might not be able to explain it, but there is a beauty that has been allocated to you. Everything about God is beautiful. In the same manner, everything about your life as a child of

God is supposed to be beautiful.

This means that your life is to be indescribable and unexplainable because of the works and hand of God in it. You need to understand that God has already allocated that life to you and the Holy Spirit of God is His ambassador to guide you into that.

So the first thing you need to do is desire your portion of glory. You cannot be satisfied with living a pitiable life. I find it interesting that many Christians encourage the sympathy of others towards them because they are void of this truth. They don't realise that the devil has robbed them of the beauty of their life. You are never to be pitied as a child of God. Any time that people start feeling sorry for you, rather than joining them and feeling sorry for yourself as well, realise that the devil is trying to steal what God has already given to you. Your portion in life is a wow not a woe.

God wants you to dwell in glory so that you can bring Him glory. People should admire you when they look at your life, whether in your home, work or academics. They should be inspired to want the life that you have. They should know that there is something more in you than in them. This way, you have an avenue to testify of God to people. That is precisely what God did with Jesus.

68

The Life God Has For You

Glorify your Son, that your Son may glorify You

John 17:1b

Thus says the Lord of hosts: 'In those days ten
men from every language of the nations shall
grasp the sleeve of a Jewish man, saying, "Let us
go with you, for we have heard that God is with
you."

Zechariah 8:23

The truth is that often believers struggle to witness boldly of their faith because there is nothing in their life that proves what they believe. Rather than being the influencer, many are influenced because the life of those they are meant to be a witness to appears to be better than theirs. Somewhere along the line, we have allowed ourselves to be convinced that our faith is in words and theories rather than demonstrations of the glory of God.

God is committed to glorifying you, but you have to be committed to a lifestyle of glory and nothing less. As long as people pity you, you cannot bring glory to the name of God. This means that you have a right to everything that Christ has that makes the world continue to celebrate Him. You didn't earn it, but it is yours because God decided to give it to you now that you are His child. Stop accepting anything other than a glorious lifestyle. I mean this in all areas of your life. Don't allow the enemy to short change you; he steals from so many believers and they don't even know it. They count it as their lot in life. God forbid! You are designed to be envied by your world. Don't stop until people begin to admire you and are inspired by your life. In simple terms, everyone that sees you should be in awe of you. Jesus said in John 17:22, And the glory which You gave Me I have given them. This tells me that God's agenda is to bestow His glory on us as His children so that the world can see His glory. You are God's avenue to the world. It is through your life that the world and those around you get to encounter the capacity and beauty of God.

We tend to master this in only one area of our lives, but if it is not in God, it should not be in you whether spiritual or physical.

CHAPTER 10

Wisdom

If any of you lacks wisdom, let him ask of God, who gives to all liberally and without reproach, and it will be given to him.

James 1:5

No one can make an impact in life without the gift of wisdom. Wisdom is one of the most important necessities for anyone who wants God to use them. The problem we have now is that believers have entirely lost this truth and so we spend all our days lifting up holy hands, praying and then expecting the magical hands of God to come and zap a change in our lives. I get frustrated when I see someone looking for a promotion at work or believing that God will make them the smartest in their class, yet they do not engage their minds to deliver the desired outcome. Why is it that we believe that because we are saved, we no longer need a mind? Our salvation does not negate the need for wisdom. Instead, it gives us the ability to become the wisest on earth. Your mind has a new capacity like no other, but if you refuse to engage this new capacity, you will keep struggling in the low places of the earth. Christians are supposed to be the wisest people on the planet because inside of us is the same mind that created the universe and keeps it fully functional century after century. Look at this scripture:

> For who has known the mind of the Lord that he may instruct Him? But we have the mind of Christ
>
> 1 Corinthians 2:16

When God made you in His image, He meant for your mental capacity to match His. There was no difference in what God could do and what Adam could do. Christ came to restore you and me back to the state of the first Adam. That restoration includes the capability of our minds.

Now examine that scripture again, who has known the mind of the Lord that he may instruct Him. God will only give the opportunity to instruct Him to those who think at His frequency. The scripture then goes on to say; we can instruct God because we now have a wisdom that matches His by our salvation through Jesus Christ. Can you see how many people are selling themselves short when it comes to their salvation? Your mind is capable of so much now that you are saved; you just have to put your new mind to work. Without this new wisdom, most of the things God wants to do through you in your generation will be a daydream because it takes a high level of wisdom to make an impact.

The Bible says in Proverbs 4:7 that wisdom is the principal thing. You cannot have a truly spiritual person that is not extremely wise. We know the scripture, iron sharpens iron (Proverbs 27:17). Well, how can someone claim to always be in the presence of God, fellowshipping with the wisest One and not have that wisdom rub off on them? It is impossible to have a real and continuous exchange and fellowship with God and not be wise. Impossible!

It will take great and novel wisdom to deliver solutions to some of the world's crises, and such wisdom is locked up in the mind of the believer. There is no challenge that you are facing now that you cannot solve. Is it an exam that is troubling you? You have the mind and wisdom of the One who created the mind that wrote that paper, so naturally, you are wiser than the lecturer. David said, you have made me wiser than my teachers, because he caught a revelation of this truth.

Rather than running away from the issues in your workplace and complaining that things are not great, engage your mind and find the solution. Solution providers are always sought after. So when it's time to make people redundant, your name will not be on the hit list. The organisation understands its need for you because of all the solutions you have provided for them. When it is time for a promotion, you will be sought after. Don't limit the ability of your mind to the education you have. This wisdom is divine and has nothing to do with your degree or lack of one. It is yours directly from heaven as part of the salvation package. You are called to the frequency of God's wisdom. Every breakthrough you are seeking, and every change that you desire is tied to solutions already living within you. There is no challenge that you cannot conquer with your mind.

Look at the story of Joseph (Genesis 41). He could bring solutions to the issues of the nation that changed not just his life but the life of his generation. I know that God has placed a dream in you that you will change your family's life, but stop daydreaming and engage your mind because that is the avenue God will use to bring that dream to pass. Without wisdom, the believer becomes irrelevant on the earth. We are still on the planet because the it needs us. I pray that as you are reading this book divine wisdom will begin to express itself in your life and turn your story around in Jesus name.

CHAPTER 11

Strength

As yet I am as strong this day as on the day that Moses sent
me; just as my strength was then, so now is my strength for
war, both for going out and for coming in

Joshua 14:11

I was sitting with my spiritual mentor one day, and he said
something that struck me because it was so accurate: "You
need this body to accomplish whatever God wills for you
to accomplish, no matter how great the vision, without the
body, it will be of no use." That is why one of the things Jesus
obtained for us on the cross was strength. Strength is necessary
to carry out our God-given vision.

As a child of God, you have the right to be healthy and
agile all the days of your life. Strength isn't merely a matter of
age, absolutely not! When I was younger, anytime I went to
Church and the pastor preached on health or strength, I would
immediately shut down mentally as I felt like it had nothing to
do with me. I was utterly ignorant of the fact that age does not

equal strength and that every time I would get a "small or slight ailment" such as a headache, it was the enemy beginning his work of chipping away at my strength.

Just because you don't have cancer or terminal disease that does not mean that every other sickness or discomfort is acceptable. Every attack against your body is contrary to the work of the cross. It is unacceptable before God because He has paid for your body to be whole always. If God is concerned about the slightest discomfort of the believer, we also must not accept them as the norm. The devil is a strategist and so is God, but unfortunately most Christians are not. We are entirely ignorant when the devil is tricking us out of our inheritance and totally blind when he steals from us.

If you accept a headache and always run to the medicine cabinet when you get one, saying, "I always get headaches"; you will have the same mindset when the enemy comes to attack you with something greater. If you do not have faith to enforce your right to health and vitality when it comes to a headache, you cannot be confident that you will be able to deal with something worse. So the enemy keeps sowing those 'small' sicknesses in our lives over the years until we become weakened in our defence against the idea of sickness. The root purpose of every illness is to kill and destroy your body so that at the end of the day the vision and purpose inside of you doesn't get fulfilled. If the devil can stop you from achieving what God has put inside of you, then He succeeds in preventing the work of God on earth that should be advanced through your life.

That is why you cannot take a careless and casual approach towards anything that plans to attack your strength. Work with God to preserve your body and not against Him. 1 Corinthians 6:19 tells us that our body is the temple of God, while 1 Corinthians 3:17 states, if anyone defiles the temple of God, God will destroy him. For the temple of God is holy, which temple you are.

God is wholly committed to destroying every plan against your strength. Strength in your body is God's priority, but it must also become yours. The Bible tells us that His body was broken for us and that by His stripes we were healed. I love this scripture because when written in Isaiah 53:5 it says we are healed but after Christ died and rose again. He obtained victory for us over the devil and all his work; the Bible says we were healed. This confirms that no sickness has a right to be found in my body.

Any sickness that you could ever have has already been removed. How therefore can you still have what has been removed? It is not possible, which means that the appearance of any sickness found in our bodies is simply that: an appearance. That is how the devil tricks many believers into creating the illness and weakness themselves with the power of their mouth.

Death and life are in the power of the tongue,
And those who love it will eat its fruit

Proverbs 18:21

Even when you feel tired, and you have work to do, speak strength to your body. Tell your body how to behave by the words of your mouth that you know have power.

CHAPTER 12

The Believer to the World

Let your light so shine before men, that they may
see your good works and glorify your Father in
heaven.

Matthew 5:16

As the world gets darker, believers have a greater opportunities to be light. We are fast entering the season when Christians will rule the world.

For the Lord shall build up Zion; He shall appear
in His glory.

Psalm 102:16

Jesus will not return until He builds up the Church: you and me, not the building. God has always been in the business of decorating His children and marking them as examples of His greatness. Understanding times and seasons in life will enable you not to fret at the crises that we observe. I want to emphasise my last statement. The evil that is going on in the world will never affect you, but only if you understand that God has put something in place to exempt you from the world's tragedy.

Evil will happen. It has been happening from the beginning of time.

> Therefore rejoice, O heavens, and you who dwell in them! Woe to the inhabitants of the earth and the sea! For the devil has come down to you, having great wrath, because he knows that he has a short time. Revelation 12:12

The anger of the devil will become more intense as we get closer to the end of time, so by the above scripture; we know that things will only get worse. Christians fear because they think that what happens on the earth applies to them too; absolutely not. John 17:16 affirms that you are in this world, but you are not of this world.

What does that mean? It means that just as an ambassador of a nation can be sent to another country, yet his status and citizenship remain aligned to his home country. The happenings of that country are not permitted to affect him. If that ambassador is affected, the wrath of his home nation will come upon the country to which he has been sent. So is the same for us. The devil sees you and because there is a seal of God on your life, saying, touch not my anointed, he has no choice but to turn away. You can only observe, but it will never affect you. Look at this scripture:

> A thousand may fall at your side, And ten thousand at your right hand; But it shall not come near you.
>
> Psalm 91:7

You have a hedge of protection around you that exempts you from the harmful happenings of this world. As it happens in heaven, so it must happen in your life because you are *in* this world, but you are from heaven; your citizenship is from heaven (Philippians 3:20). You need to be conscious of this truth: you can see it, but it will not come near you.

There is going to be a clear distinction between the children of God and the rest of the world, so this is not the time to be 'one foot in, one foot out' with your faith. Dive in with all your heart, give everything that you are to God and let there be no question as to what side you stand on. I believe that Christians are in for the best of times and you cannot afford to miss out.

Can you imagine serving God for many years and just before it's payday, you fall away? That's the strategy of the devil; to make believers weary of their faith and their walk just before God is about to decorate the Church. Don't allow anything to remove your name from that list.

> Then you shall again discern between the righteous and the wicked, between one who serves God and one who does not serve Him.
>
> Malachi 3:18

Take the children of Israel, the curses came upon the children of Egypt but were not permitted to go near the Israelites. If you observe the winds of the sky and the natural occurrences and use it as an indicator of your life, you will not seize the opportunities this season has for you.

When the economic crisis happened, many feared they would lose their jobs. However, in that same season believers, who knew they were exempted, were gaining promotions, while others were growing wealth. I remember that in that time, I handled more money than ever before in my life. It wasn't only me that had such a great testimony in that period. I would hear believers say, "My workplace was making people redundant, and I declared that it would not affect me and my whole department was let go, but not me." We are in charge of the earth, so it must happen to us as we demand. Stop acting like a subject and take your royal position, this is your territory!

I get excited for the Christian community in every nation to make waves and to be real contributors to society and that day is fast approaching. I see the manifestation of the sons of God (Romans 8:19) coming on the earth, but I pray that you are a part of that happening. There is a rising of a new world just like the world the Israelites lived in Egypt called Goshen. The Goshen experience is God's intent for His children as the world gets darker. I love it when the Bible tells us that when men are cast down, then thou shalt say, there is lifting up (Job 22:29, KJV). This is not just a declaration of faith, it is speaking of the reality of having a positive testimony and life experience in the midst of others saying the opposite. Isn't that what will make people ask you to show them your God? (Zechariah 8:23: Show us your God for we have seen that He is with you.)

The world will not attribute glory to God solely because of our speech and rhetoric. Talk is cheap. You say, "God is great," they are going to say, "Prove it." God has always known that the world will demand proof and He has always provided that proof that by signs, wonders and miracles in the life His children. You are not excluded from experiencing signs, wonders, and miracles. Frustration awaits those who always claim that God is something that they have never experienced. If you refuse to ask God earnestly for something, how can you experience it? God is up to amazing things in this season; cry with a desperate heart to be a part of it. Whatever our great God is doing, He can do in you too.

I once had a dream that I have never been able to shake off. In the dream, Jesus was passing over the earth and distributing gifts to men. I caught that He was doing this and began crying out desperately for Him not to pass me by until I too received a gift from Him. This dream is an exact image of my personality and attitude in my faith. If I see that God is doing something, I will not rest until I am a part of it and that I too experience what He is doing. So many Christians are satisfied with hearing other people's testimonies and experiences but deep down do not expect for the same to be replicated in their lives. What a shame it is to have the opportunity from God to live an unexplainable life and instead you choose to live a life like the masses. If they suffer, you are not supposed to suffer. If they are struggling, you are not supposed to be struggling. Fight your way into the believer's world because that is where you are to live. There is a world within this world being built by Jesus on the earth. We can live in it and have incredible experiences that are opposite to the negative occurrences of this world. However, you have to live out of the consciousness that you are not of this world. God's children are rising. You have to force yourself to be included among the rising stars.

CHAPTER 13

When It Seems Like Your Faith Is Failing

Therefore take up the whole armor of God, that
you may be able to withstand in the evil day, and
having done all, to stand.

Ephesians 6:13

One day a young lady said to me with great dismay that she didn't quite understand how her mother could devote all of her life to a belief in God, yet face such continuous struggles without hope. This young girl's faith was shaken because somewhere in life she had been led to believe that a walk with God made life rosy without any challenges or struggles. Quite the contrary, all through the Bible we see great men of faith continuously tested and challenged. However, the battles they won have become the hallmark of their greatness. If we are to follow their examples and seek to be admired in our communities like they were, then the only thing that I can guarantee you is that your faith will be tested. A saying that sums this up, and that is true in its entirety, is "It is not unspiritual to be challenged, but it is unscriptural to be defeated." So though God has set for us His children this glorious life with significant benefits, there is someone out there called the devil who wants to question your right to live in it and steal all you have been given.

What happens with many Christians is that once the devil challenges our faith, we give up. We become defeated and lose hope. This is what your enemy the devil wants: your faith. Every challenge you face is designed to destroy or steal your faith. It is by the avenue of your faith that you will live in everything that God has promised you. The challenge is not the focus; the focus is your faith. This is the reason you will find that once it seems like one challenge is over another arises. Remember the scripture when Jesus spoke about a demon being cast out of a person? The demon comes back with more demons (greater challenge), looking for an opportunity to overcome the individual (Matthew 12:43-45). So you have to defend your faith with all your strength. It is all about your faith! If you stop believing, you will remove yourself from the life God has prepared for you. You cannot give up just because you are challenged. It may be tough, it may seem like the world is closing in on you, but you just cannot give up.

In fact, this is the time that you should believe even the more. Dig your heels deeper into all that you have believed before. Like Abraham, though its looks contrary to everything around you, all you know to be right for you, you have to hope in spite of the fact that it looks like there is nothing to expect.

I remember being pregnant with my second son, Isaiah. Every single stage was contrary to what I knew to be my portion in Christ. I knew I wasn't to bring forth child in pain; I knew that the blessing of the Lord makes rich and adds no sorrow. However, I was in severe pain throughout my pregnancy. I had a choice before me: to question God and feel sorry for myself, or to fight and win over my enemy, the devil.

It turned out that my decision would be a matter of life or death. This wasn't simply about having an easy pregnancy. The devil wanted me dead. I felt severe pain every day. It restricted my movement and threatened to steal my life and that of my child. Now I could hold myself back by whining, or I could choose not to be distracted by the pain and fight for my life. Well, I am alive and have written this book, so you know what I chose.

I remember sitting in the hospital with my husband. The consultant looked at us and said, "There is a strong chance that you will lose your life or the life of the child, but our priority is to save yours." Immediately I felt afraid right to the core of my soul. Just before I became pregnant, I had lost a close friend of mine due to her pregnancy, so the words of the consultant felt so real to me. But look at the word I used; FELT. It felt real, but it wasn't. How did I know that? Before I became pregnant, I spoke to God, and He told me that. He would give me a child and that He by Himself would preserve my life. God knew that deep down, the experience of my friend had yielded a negative impact on my life and as I came before Him, He spoke to the fear that was inside me. So, when the doctors said what they said, the voice of God rose up inside me. My feelings and emotions were intense but His voice and His word to me was stronger.

The issue with many is that the challenge and their emotions are stronger than the voice of God to them. Whenever you find yourself in a trial, don't allow the chaos to push you away from the voice of God. Instead, take that confusion to the feet of your master. Cast your cares on the Lord, Jesus genuinely does care for you.

Your decision to hear God in the midst of your challenge will birth faith in you that will triumph over every difficulty. Every morning I woke up to the reality of intense pain reminding me of the medical report that there was a high probability that I would die. However, I focussed on a more significant truth: the integrity of the words that God spoke to me. No matter how real that pain was, I did not allow that pain to speak into my life; I did not allow myself to get tempted into a conversation with the appearance of death. Instead, I conversed with God's word.

You must learn to converse with the promises God has given you. Keep them before you and allow them to birth great faith in you because that faith is what will cause you to continue on your journey until you reach the promised land.

The day I was giving birth, the hospital had gathered together their most senior team, and they were prepared for the worst. However God dismantled that team, none of them could be found; stuck in one thing or the other. I remember holding Isaiah in my hands and everyone laughing where there was supposed to be chaos. The devil has no power, so instead, he puts distractions in your path to cause you to walk away from God promises. But know this, as long as you don't give up on your journey to the promised land, everything God has promised will come to pass.

Even when it seems like the pressure is going to break you, know that you are stronger and that it won't break you, you will endure it, and in the end, you will win. No temptation has overtaken you except such as is common to man; but God is faith-

The Life God Has For You

ful, who will not allow you to be tempted beyond what you are able, but with the temptation will also make the way of escape, that you may be able to bear it. (1 Corinthians 10:13)